PROJECTS
WITH
PAPER
COILS
AND
SCROLLS

Easy Quillery

EVA V. AMIDON
ILLUSTRATED BY CHARLES H. AMIDON, JR.

William Morrow and Company   New York 1977

1   2   3   4   5   6   7   8   9   10

Library of Congress Cataloging in Publication Data

Amidon, Eva V.
  Easy quillery.

  SUMMARY: Twelve paper filigree projects with an introduction to techniques and suggestions for other projects.
    1. Paper quillwork—Juvenile literature. [1. Paper quillwork.
  2. Handicraft]   I. Amidon, Charles H.
  TT870.A47   745.54   77-6463
  ISBN 0-688-22130-0
  ISBN 0-688-32130-5 lib. bdg.

Contents

What Quillery Is

Centuries ago some creative person found that narrow strips of paper could be rolled into coils or bent into bugs, birds, flowers, and fancy scrolls. So clever were those early paper artists that when their designs were painted with gold, they were hard to distinguish from the expensive metalwork called "filigree" that the wealthy had on their furniture and jewelry boxes.

Then artistic people began experimenting with colored paper and liked the bright effects. They realized that objects did not have to look like gold to be pretty. In Europe this paper rolling was called "paper filigree." About 1700 it became known as quilling, or quillery because the American ladies who introduced the craft to the Colonies rolled their coils around the quill, or base end, of a feather.

In some of our eastern American museums you can find candle sconces with intricately quilled, glassed-in backgrounds of birds and flowers. Colonial ladies made tiny crimps in paper strips by hand. They glued these crimped strips around small bird cutouts to form frames. They filled these frames with exceptionally tiny scrolls. Delicate quilled borders surrounded the arrangements of flowers and birds.

But few colonists could afford special paper just for craft activities, and since no paper was wasted, it's quite likely that all Colonial quilling was done with used paper. Today precut strips of colored paper can be bought at art-supply stores. Special tools can also be bought. However, we have a bountiful supply of suitable weights and colors in the paper that we throw away. Many of our household items can become tools. Therefore, quilling can be an inexpensive hobby for anyone who wants to try it.

Quillery can be very simple or very complicated, depending on the quiller's skill. You will find that the projects in this book are relatively simple. Sprinkled throughout the book are cues for using the designs in different ways, cues about color and size, cues for objects to decorate, and cues about tools. By the time you have made a few of the projects, you will be creating your own original designs and passing along your cues to others.

Getting Organized

Quilling makes use of small objects, such as needles and pins, toothpicks, and tweezers. So it is very important to have an adequate storage box for your tools. A suit or dress box will serve the purpose. Inside it you can glue or tape a smaller box for tools and materials. Candle boxes are ideal to keep paper strips in. Egg-carton sections can hold leftover paper coils. The bottom of your box can hold a supply of paper.

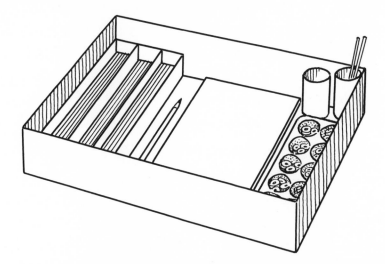

As you progress with a few projects, you will become aware of objects and materials that will be useful for future projects. Such materials should go into your box. Greeting cards and their colored envelopes, gift wrappings, and even colored papers covered with writing or printing are useful.

A small drawing board, or even a heavy piece of cardboard, will make a good working surface and will prevent scratches and glue spots on a desk or table.

Curly-cue: Part of being organized when you are a quiller is keeping your hands and tools clean and free from glue. Beside your storage box keep a small plastic bowl for holding a damp sponge or a piece of folded, damp paper towel. Every time your fingers touch glue, sponge them off.

As you finish each project, wipe off your tools so you will be organized for the next one.

TOOLS YOU NEED

Needle, 1 mm in diameter
Needle, 2 mm in diameter

Round pencil, 6 mm in diameter
Soft (#2) pencils
Black felt-tip pen
Metric ruler
Sharp scissors
Craft knife
Paper punch
Tweezers

Six wooden snap clothespins
Wooden toothpicks
Small bottle caps
Stapler
Plastic jar lids

Curly-cues: When a needle drops on the floor, it's sometimes hard to find it. To help you locate your needles quickly, attach a key tag to them.

A corsage pin is about 1 mm in diameter and is handy to use for winding because the knob helps you hold it. Other smooth, round objects can be used also. However, the project directions in this book will list those given above.

MATERIALS YOU NEED

Heavy bond typing paper, new or used
Lined notebook-filler paper,
    new or used, white or pastel
New or used notepaper and its envelopes
Construction paper
Bright-colored ads and meeting notices
Brown kraft paper (flat parts of grocery bags)
Pieces of cardboard and poster board
Cardboard gift boxes
Backs of used greeting cards
Tracing paper

Cupcake papers
White craft glue
Masking tape
Blocks of foam plastic, such as Styrofoam
Felt scraps
Fabric scraps in plain colors
Sewing trimming and rickrack braid
Glitter
Used greeting-card messages and scenes
Wooden craft sticks
Plastic drinking straws
Cardboard tubing 4 cm in diameter

Curly-cue: Construction paper comes in many colors and in different weights. It is a wise selection if you wish to create a large, heavy-looking design. However, it does fade, a disadvantage to remember if you wish your project to look lovely forever. It is sometimes stiff but will coil quite easily if you scrape each strip over a scissors blade first.

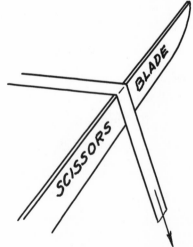

CUTTING AND STORING STRIPS

Most of the projects in this book suggest strips about 3 mm, 4 mm, or 5 mm wide. Each project has drawings to show the actual widths and lengths of the strips.

Most beginners practice with strips about 5 mm wide, and after a few practice projects, they find they can work just as easily with narrower strips. Practice cutting some different kinds of paper into strips. Cut some that are 3 mm, 4 mm, and 5 mm wide.

Most projects call for strips short enough to be cut from notebook-size paper. To get longer strips, overlap two short strips, glue them, and allow them to dry thoroughly before you coil them. When making long strips line up the lower edges with a ruler before the glue sets.

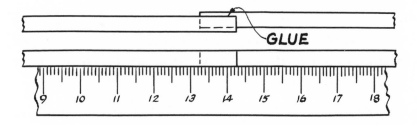

These strips must form a *straight* line, or you will not be able to coil them properly.

When you are ready to begin some of the projects in this book, cut only the strips you need for the project you are doing. A large pile of precut strips can easily become tangled or bent.

Sharp scissors with blades about 8 cm long are best

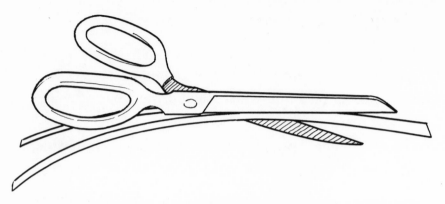

for cutting strips. At first your scissor-cut strips may be uneven in places. However, some uneven cutting adds an interesting texture to flowers, leaves, and birds. To begin with, cut only one thickness of paper at a time. Expert cutters usually cut no more than two or three sheets at a time. If you have a paper cutter to use, you will also discover that it is unwise to cut more than two sheets at a time because the sheets underneath tend to slide. To make very narrow strips, cut wider ones in half.

An adult can cut a generous supply of strips for you very quickly by using a sharp craft knife, a cutting board, and a metal straight-edged ruler. This is an excellent way for an adult to cut straight strips, but it is not advisable for you.

HOW TO MAKE COILS

The Round Closed Coil

Since the paper coil is the basis for all quillery, it is a good idea to practice making some before you begin your

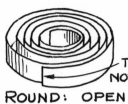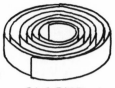

ROUND: OPEN   CLOSED   SOLID

TAIL NOT GLUED

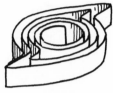

PINCHED: PETAL   LEAF   LEAF

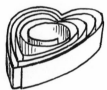

PINCHED: TRIANGLE, TULIP   HEART   SQUARE

SCROLLS: EYEGLASS   HEART   V   OPEN

S

PUSHED-OUT, PULLED-OUT COILS   FRAME, CYLINDRICAL COILS

first project. As you can see by looking at the drawing on page 13, showing the types of coils, there are a number of possible shapes. The round closed coil is the most important because so many other coils are made from it. Most beginners find that a large needle (2 mm in diameter) is easy to handle.

Cut some horizontal strips 5 mm wide from typing paper and make some closed coils. Here is how you do it:

1. Moisten your thumb and your index finger slightly, and place the tip of the paper strip on your finger as shown. Then lay the needle on the strip close to the end of the strip.

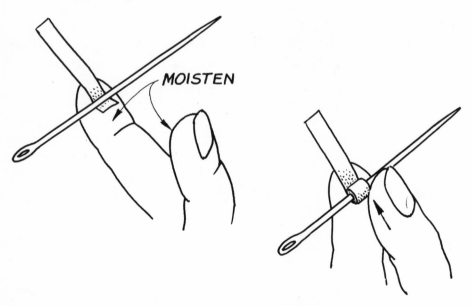

2. With your thumb bend the tip of the strip up against the needle and push the needle forward, making sure that the paper rolls around the needle.

14

3. Roll the winder to the tip of your finger, return your thumb and the needle to the starting point and roll again. Repeat this action until the strip is fully wound.

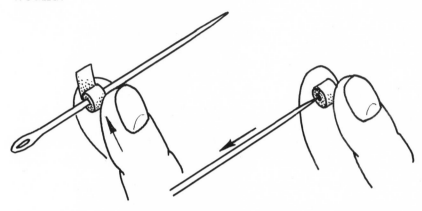

4. When the strip has been carefully wound, slip it off the needle. Be careful not to let it unroll.

5. With a wooden toothpick place a dot of glue on the strip's inner surface near the tail.

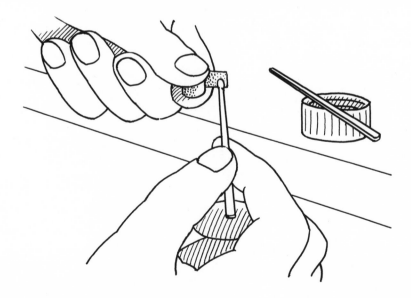

6. Keeping your fingers around the coil, let it slowly spring open until it is about dime size. Now press the glue spot against the side of the coil, and hold it a few seconds until the glue sets.

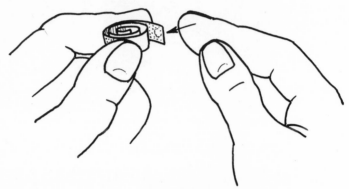

All experts do not hold their needle and paper the way described in steps #1, #2, and #3. You can roll the paper coil toward you between your left thumb and forefinger, while rolling the needle in the same direction with your right hand, as shown in the drawing. Or you can discover the way that works best for you.

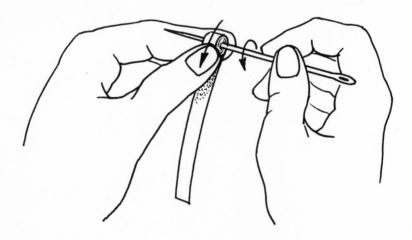

Curly-cue: As you practice making the round closed coil, you can create something useful. Fold a piece of heavy paper (7 cm by 14 cm) in half. Roll seven round coils and glue them on the top to make a simple gift enclosure card.

The Pinched Coil

To form a pinched closed coil, first construct a round, closed coil. Then pinch one or both sides, as shown. Be

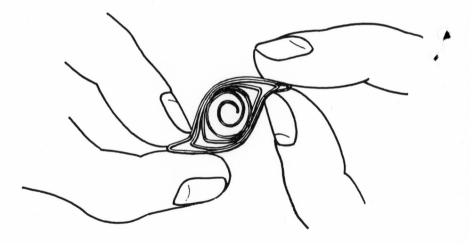

careful not to spoil the center design when pinching. You want the coils to remain round in the center!

There are five factors that determine the design within a pinched closed coil:

1. the diameter of the winding tool
2. the size of the paper strip
3. the weight of the paper strip
4. the diameter of the coil before it is pinched
5. the number of times the coil is pinched

Try pinching a round closed coil into a triangle by pinching it at three equally spaced points. Make a fourth pinch between two of these, and you have a tulip shape. Add a stem and blades and you have one tulip. Four or five of these coils around a center produce a flower something like a bachelor's button.

By pinching a round closed coil with your left hand and holding this point while you push against the coil

on the opposite side with your right index finger, you can form a heart. This coil can be a flower by itself or be used with others to form a blossom.

Try pinching a round closed coil into an eye-shaped leaf coil. By creasing it on the top and on the bottom, you can form a square. Several squares make a nice border. Five or six around a center can be a flower.

The Solid Coil

Solid coils have many uses. Small, short ones arranged in a circle can form a flower. They can be glued on upright or in a horizontal position. Tall ones that make tiny cylinders can look like buds around a flower. As you practice these, make a place card.

Use a 2-mm needle as a winding tool and cut some strips 10 cm long. Choose a color you like. Wind eight strips into round closed coils. Choose the best six coils, and glue them in a circle on a small rectangle of heavy paper. With a toothpick dab glue under each coil and where it touches the next coil. Make two green round solid coils and place one on each side of the flower for leaves. Make one card with the cylinders upright and one with the cylinders glued on sideways.

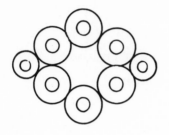 

Solid coils can be noses for clowns or animals, or they can be eyes. If you glue the coils shut leaving a little end free, you have eyelashes.

To make an eye bright and saucy, wind a solid black coil for the pupil and tightly wind a narrower white strip around it. When you glue on the white outer strip, have its lower edge flush with the black strip. This makes the pupil higher than the white of the eye. On a gingerbread man this kind of an eye really looks like a raisin!

The Scroll-type Coil

Scrolls are useful for filling in open spaces and for building border designs. Several projects in this book suggest using scrolls of different kinds.

The S scroll is made by loosely rolling one end of a short strip toward the center and then loosely rolling the opposite end away from the center. Do not glue the tails. Use strips of 6 cm or less to make them.

The eyeglasses scroll is best made from strips about 5 cm long. For this one, roll both ends toward the center.

The heart scroll is made by folding the strip in half and then rolling each end toward the center. Use a 5-cm strip to practice this one.

The V scroll has many uses. It can be part of a filled-in design. It can be a nose and eye combination for a small funny face. It can be antennae for insects. It can be small flower stems.

To make it, fold the strip in half and then roll each end outward.

Round open scrolls are very useful for filling in spaces. These use strips as short as 2 cm and 3 cm.

The Pulled-out Coil

Pulled-out coils, or tendrils, are spiral coils often used as fill-in material for fruit and flower designs. This same kind of coil would make good hair for a rag doll or a clown.

To make a tendril, twist a strip 6 cm long around a needle so that it forms a spiral along the needle. If the strip is wound tightly and slipped off gently, it will remain a spiral.

The Pushed-out Coil

Domelike coils can make a good center for a large daisy. They can be clowns' noses. If they are large enough, they can be clowns' hats . . . or even hats for witches.

Start with a strip 5 mm wide and about 50 cm long. Roll it around a 1-mm needle into a tight closed coil. Do not let it spring at all. Glue its tail and allow the coil to dry. Then slowly and gently push up the center of the coil with your thumb. Once the center has been raised, it can be kept in position by spreading glue inside the coil and letting it dry.

Sizing Coils

It is easier to make a set of identical round coils than of any other shape. Therefore, if you want a matched set of pinched coils, first wind a set of round coils of the same diameter, let them stand while the glue sets, and then pinch them all at once.

A simple jig makes it easy to size round coils exactly. (A jig is a box, plate, or open frame designed to hold an object while you work on it.) Suppose you need a set of six dime-sized round coils. You might make a jig in one of the following ways.

1. Place a dime on a piece of thick cardboard or soft wood and stick four common pins around it. Use the dime to make six identical jigs, each consisting of four pins.

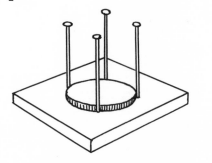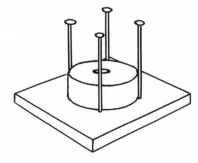

2. You may find bottle caps that just fit around the dime. If each cap is too deep for the width of the coil you want to wind, roll a "filler coil" and glue it in the bottom of the cap.

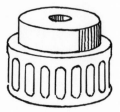 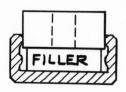

3. A wooden frame similar to a small ladder provides square openings for a matched set of coils. Lay two narrow craft sticks on a flat surface with a dime between them at each end. Glue a wooden toothpick across the top surfaces of the sticks near one end, on either side of

one dime. When the glue sets, remove the dime at that end and use it as a spacer to glue additional toothpicks along the craft sticks like the rungs of a ladder. Seven toothpicks will give you six square openings. Then glue two craft sticks on top of the toothpicks directly over the two original sticks.

Curly-cues: An advantage of the pin jig (#1) or the frame jig (#3) is that the tail of the paper strip may be glued while the coil is in the jig.

Shirt buttons and coins make handy circles to help you size coils. Most patterns in this book call for either 1-cm coils or dime-sized coils.

I cm	1.3 cm	1.75 cm	2.1 cm	2.4 cm
BUTTONS		DIME	NICKEL	QUARTER

GLUES

There are several kinds of glue. Many of those that work well with plastic have fumes that are harmful if inhaled. Such glues must be used in a well-ventilated room. Since quilling involves such tiny bits of paper, it's not practical to work near any open windows where a sudden breeze could greatly disturb your work. White craft glue is safe, inexpensive, and easily available, and it has no harmful odors.

To make your supply last longer, pour a little into a bottle cap and close your glue bottle. Use a wooden toothpick to apply the small dabs of glue you need for your quillery.

Even this small amount of glue will not dry up if you set the bottle cap inside a small plastic container with an airtight lid when you are not dipping into it.

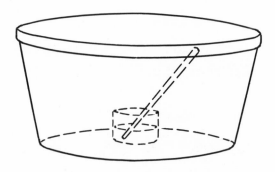

One disadvantage of white craft glue is that it does not adhere well to all kinds of plastic surfaces. If you wish to place a design on a small area of a smooth plastic object, add bits of masking tape to the area to hold a design. Glue your design over the masking tape.

But because white glue does not adhere to smooth plastic jar lids, they make an excellent surface to assemble designs on. Suppose you are building a flower that will rest on a post rather than a background surface. You will need to build the whole flower first and then glue it on the post. Lay your first petal on the lid, and touch each side of it with glue where another petal will touch it. As you tuck each petal in place, dab its side with glue, being careful not to let glue drip down onto the lid. Let the assembled flower dry in place on the lid. If any glue has dripped down, gently pry the flower loose. It will peel off easily.

TRACING PATTERNS FROM A BOOK

The page of a book can be damaged if a picture is traced with carbon paper, with sharp tools, or if too much pressure is used.

Lay a piece of tracing paper over the pattern you wish to copy. Tuck the paper deep between the pages to avoid slippage. Hold the tracing paper in place with one hand while you lightly trace the pattern outline with your other hand. Use a #2 pencil because it is soft and will not leave ridges in the book. Do not press down hard. Do not use paper clips around the edge of the page because they can crease the page, and, of course, do not use tape.

Once you have lightly sketched the outline, then remove the tracing paper from the book and lay it on your desk or table. Darken and sharpen your outline now.

To transfer your outline to another surface, turn

your tracing over. On the underside your pattern will show in reverse. Again, using the #2 pencil, blacken the page with a horizontal zigzag motion until all the lines are well covered.

Turn the paper right side up, and lay it on your project. This time you can bear down a little as you trace. Lift the tracing off the surface of your project, and darken your lines if you need to.

A second way to transfer a pattern is to use carbon paper. However, the smudges often left by it cannot be erased. Soft pencil smudges do erase easily.

Store your tracing patterns in envelopes so they will not smudge your other art supplies.

MAKING A TEMPLATE

If you are going to make more than one item, you can save time by making a template to trace around. In such a case, follow the tracing cues above, and transfer your outline to a piece of light cardboard. Cut out your pattern (template). It should be kept in an envelope to protect it from bending.

Pincushion

Make one for a gift and another to hold the needles and pins you will use in your quillery.

The one in the picture is 2 cm thick. Your pincushion does not need to be a rectangle. It could be square or circular, but it should be at least 2 cm thick. This pincushion would look equally nice with plain-edged felt.

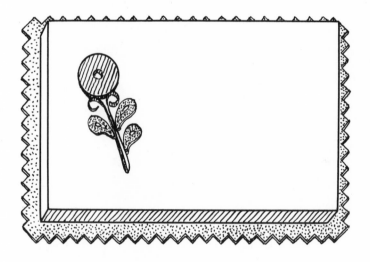

What You Need
Smooth block of foamed plastic about 8 cm by 5 cm
Piece of felt slightly larger than the foam block
Needle 2 mm in diameter
Notepaper strips 5 mm wide,
    the lengths and colors stated on the next page:

FLOWER: 1 RED 15 cm

LEAVES: 3 GREEN 12 cm

STEM: 1 GREEN 10 cm

What You Do

1. Spread glue on the underside of the foam slab, and press it on the center of your felt base.

2. Coil the red blossom strip into a round closed coil 1 cm in diameter. Glue it in place near the upper left corner of the block.

3. Fold the green stem strip in half, and make a V-shaped coil by rolling each end outward until the stem is the desired length.

4. Using a toothpick, spread glue inside the stem fold, under the end coils, and under the stem itself. Press the stem on the block under the flower.

5. Make the leaf coils by pinching round closed coils. As you glue each one on the block, dab glue under it and on its side where it will touch the stem. By gluing leaves on both sides of a stem, you strengthen it and keep it upright.

Pendants

Quilled pendants look best if they are no larger than 5 cm in diameter. Directions are given for three styles, all of which feature easy-to-find materials.

CARDBOARD CIRCLE

What You Need
Cardboard circle about 4 cm in diameter
Narrow rickrack braid about 14 cm long
Neck cord or chain about 50 cm long
1-mm needle
2-mm needle
Plastic straw
Notepaper strips 5 mm wide as shown:

FLOWERS : 3 RED 15 cm

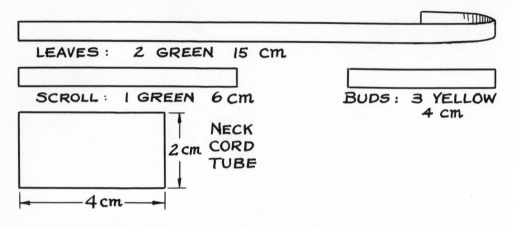

LEAVES : 2 GREEN 15 cm

SCROLL : 1 GREEN 6 cm

BUDS : 3 YELLOW 4 cm

NECK CORD TUBE

2 cm

4 cm

What You Do

1. Using the 2-mm needle, wind the three red strips into round closed coils for the flowers. Glue them on the circle.

2. Using the 2-mm needle, make the leaves and scroll. Glue them in place around the flowers.

3. Using the 1-mm needle, roll the yellow strips into tiny tight cylinders and glue their ends. Glue these buds in place.

4. You are now ready to add the rickrack border. It works best if you glue only part of the braid at a time. Begin at the bottom of the circle, and with a toothpick,

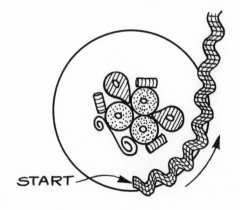

START

carefully spread glue along the edge as far as the "3 o'clock" position. Now press the braid in the line of glue, letting the braid extend slightly over the cut edge. Let this section dry and then do the next quarter of the circle.

5. Using the plastic straw as a winder, roll the white paper rectangle into a tight cylinder and glue its tail. Slip it off the straw, and glue it on the back of the quilled cardboard circle in a horizontal position.

6. Thread your neck cord through the tube and tie its ends. Place a little glue on the knot, and pull it inside the tube where it can hide.

PLASTIC PILL-BOTTLE CAP

What You Need
Plastic pill-bottle cap,
    5 cm in diameter and 5 mm deep
White paper circle 4.6 cm in diameter
Flat cord or ribbon for neck

What You Do

1. Near the top of the cap make two vertical slashes with the tip of a paring knife. Make them about 1 cm long and 1 cm apart.

2. Thread a ribbon end through each slash. Add two bits of masking tape to keep the ends flat against the inside of the cap, but before you tape the ends flat, make certain that the ribbon has not spiraled. Add three or four more bits of tape around the inside of the cap. Glue will stick to this tape and hold your paper insert inside the frame.

3. Spread glue on the back of the white paper circle, and press it inside the cap against the masking-tape bits.

4. You can add the same design that you used on the cardboard circle or you can change it. If your cap is red, you will at least want to make the flowers a different color.

EYEGLASS LENSES

What You Need

Select a lens that is symmetrical. It can be clear or tinted, glass or plastic. Sun lenses of green or brown can look elegant with all-white quillery. Opticians often have discarded eyeglass lenses that they will give away.

What You Do

1. You can glue a tube on the back of the lens, as you did on the cardboard circle. It will show through, but your quillery will hide it. Or you can glue a piece of flat ribbon on the back (along the top edge), and your border will hide it.

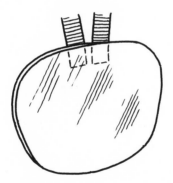

2. To hide scratches or the magnification lines of bifocals, you can cover the top of the lens with finely woven fabric. To do this, lay the lens on the fabric and trace around it. Cut it out carefully. With a toothpick spread a thin line of glue around the edge of the lens, and lay the cloth in place. When dry, hide its edges with a rickrack border. Do your quillery on top.

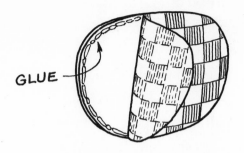

GLUE

Curly-cues: Tiny-checked pastel gingham makes an appealing background for lens pendants. Young people like blue denim glued under a clear lens. Red-and-white quillery looks appropriate on denim.

Since lenses are smooth, white glue needs several minutes of drying time. So it is important to add a small section of border braid at a time and allow each section time to dry. Otherwise, the preceding sections will slide off. Tiny rickrack braid makes such a dainty frame that the time you wait is worthwhile.

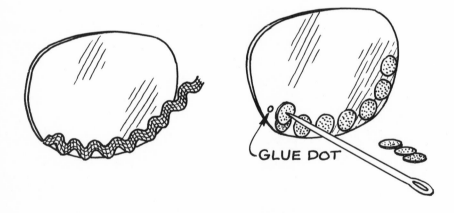

GLUE DOT

Paper punch cutouts make a suitable frame too. They are easy to add. With a toothpick place a series of glue dots around a section of the edge. Gently pierce a punch cutout with a needle point, hold it over the glue dot and push it off the needle and into place with another needle.

For a few cents you can buy a pin back at a craft store and make a pin rather than a pendant.

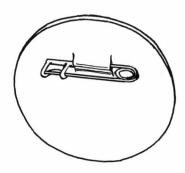

Bracelets with Quillery

A wooden tongue depressor can be teased into an open-backed bracelet for an adult (6 cm in diameter), or you can make an open-backed bracelet or a circular one in any size by cutting a cross section from a soft, pliable plastic bottle.

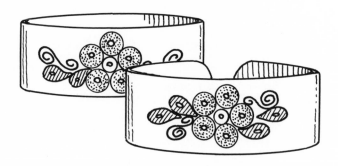

A PLASTIC-BOTTLE BRACELET

If you can slip your hand through a 5-cm circle, you can make a circular bracelet with a straight-sided plastic bottle 5 cm in diameter. Or you can use a 4-cm bottle to make an open-backed bracelet, since it does not have to slide over the wide part of your hand. To hold quilling, a bracelet should be at least 2 cm wide. While a 3-cm-wide bracelet can hold larger designs, this width does not look very nice on a short or chubby arm. An adult with long, thin arms might like a bracelet as wide as 3.5 cm.

What You Need

Plastic bottle of suitable diameter

Masking tape

What You Do

1. Mark off the desired width for your bracelet with two parallel strips of masking tape.

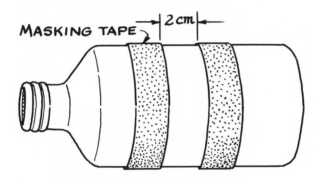

2. Before you cut the plastic, very carefully and slowly scratch grooves with a knife. Use the taped edges as a guide. Force the tip of the knife through one of the scratched lines, and slowly "saw" along the line. Many

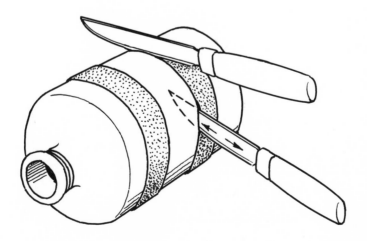

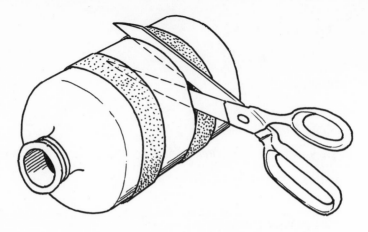

cylindrical containers can be cut with scissors after a slit has been made with a knife. Scissors are safest.

3. If you wish an open-backed bracelet, make a vertical scissor cut in your circlet and round the four corners.

Curly-cue: A piece of wood dowel jammed into the mouth of the plastic bottle will give you a better "handle" when cutting with a knife.

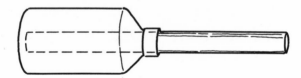

A TONGUE-DEPRESSOR BRACELET

Your drugstore will sell several wooden tongue depressors for a few cents. A stick 2 cm wide and 15 cm long is the best size for a bracelet. Narrow craft sticks will crack.

What You Need

A tongue depressor

A straight-sided, circular container
 with a diameter of 6 cm, such as a jelly jar

An adult to help with the first two steps below
 because boiling water is hazardous

What You Do

1. Drop a tongue depressor into a small pan of boiling water. Turn off the heat.

2. Remove the stick after it has soaked twenty minutes.

3. While it is warm and wet, force the stick into the straight-sided jar. Force it against the sides so its shape will be as circular as possible.

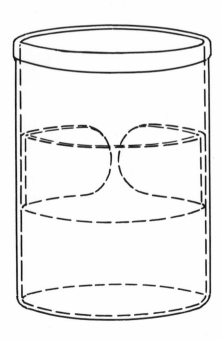

4. Allow the bracelet to dry in the jar for twenty-four hours. Once completely dry, it will retain its shape.

Curly-cue: To protect your hands you may wish to wear gloves. Or two pairs of pliers can be used to bend the hot stick slowly into a circular shape.

A BRACELET DESIGN

On most wrists a simple design looks the best. It should only extend over the part of the bracelet that covers the back of the wrist, where it will be protected from bumps. The design does not have to be symmetrical, but it should have a balance of color and an even distribution of large and small coils.

If your bracelet is plastic, before you add the decoration place a small oval of masking tape on the area where you wish to glue quillery. (White craft glue adheres well to masking tape.)

This design is sturdy and will stand lots of bumps. It looks nice on a wide bracelet too. If you wish, you may put two flowers on a wide bracelet and tuck in two or three more leaves and scrolls for balance.

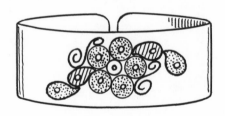

What You Need

1-mm needle

Construction paper strips 2 mm wide,
   the lengths and colors shown below:

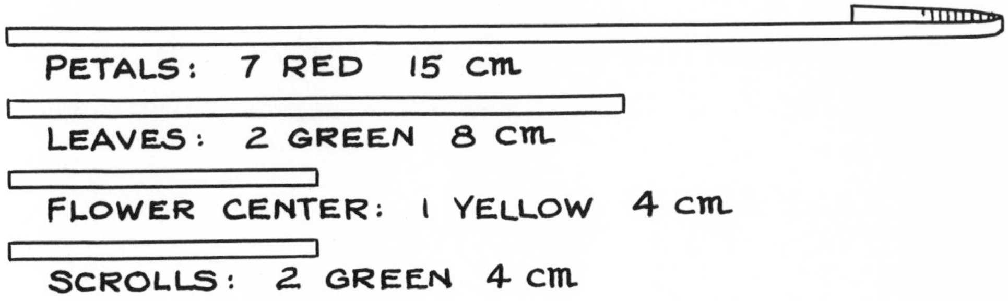

PETALS: 7 RED   15 CM

LEAVES: 2 GREEN   8 CM

FLOWER CENTER: 1 YELLOW   4 CM

SCROLLS: 2 GREEN   4 CM

What You Do

1. Wind the yellow strip around the 1-mm needle, and glue its tail so that it forms a tight closed coil. Dab glue under it, and position it in the exact center of the design area.

2. Wind five of the red strips into solid coils, and glue them around the yellow center. As you add each coil, dab glue under it and on its sides where it will touch other coils.

3. Make the other two red coils. Dab glue under them, and position them 1 cm away from the center flower, one on each side for balance.

4. Make the two green leaves and the two green scrolls, and glue them between the central flower and the two single red coils.

5. Allow the bracelet to dry overnight before wearing it.

Napkin Ring

This napkin ring is made from a section of cardboard tubing, such as the ones paper towels or toilet tissue are rolled on. It is covered with tan wrapping paper, which makes an attractive background for yellow. You may prefer other colors.

What You Need
Cardboard cylinder 4 cm in diameter and 6 cm long
Piece of brown wrapping paper 6 cm by 16 cm
30-cm strip of tiny yellow rickrack braid
1-mm needle
Tiny scrap of orange paper for flower center
Notepaper strips 4 mm wide as follows:

PETALS: 6 YELLOW   14 cm

LEAVES: 2 GREEN   11 cm

44

SCROLLS : 2 GREEN 4 cm

What You Do

1. Before you cut your tubing, measure in 6 cm from one end of the cylinder and make a pencil dot. Do this four times to get four dots 6 cm from the end. Stretch a tight rubber band through all four dots to serve as a cutting guide.

2. Carefully pierce the tube with the tip of a craft knife or a paring knife, and slowly and carefully "saw" around the tube.

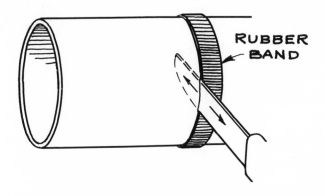

RUBBER BAND

3. Spread a very thin layer of glue on the background paper and press it on the tubing, keeping the edges as straight and smooth as possible. Think of the seam as the back of the napkin ring.

4. Wind the six petals and expand them to a circle 8 mm in diameter. Then pinch them.

5. Make a pencil point in the exact center of the front of the napkin holder, and glue the petals around this

point. Dab glue under each petal and where it touches others.

6. Add an orange paper-punch cutout on the center of the flower.

7. Assemble the leaves and the two green scrolls. Glue them between the petals where you think they look best.

8. You are now ready to glue on the edge braid. You want it to come right to the nice straight edge you made, but not extend over it. (If it were hanging over the edge, it would become wrinkled and bent when napkins were pushed into the ring.) Beginning at the back and along one edge, make a thin line of glue one quarter of the way around the tube with a toothpick. Beginning at the back, carefully press a small section of the rickrack braid along the line of glue. Add the remaining braid in this same manner, working carefully to keep it straight.

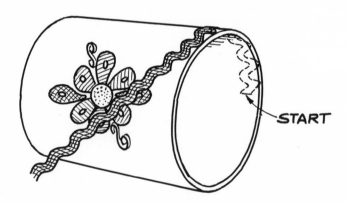

START

Curly-cue: If some adult you love enjoys entertaining, a set of matched napkin rings would be a welcome gift.

Sewing Kit

This kit for holding emergency sewing tools makes an attractive gift. It has a sturdy design that can withstand the shuffling and bumping it will get in a purse.

What You Need
Lightweight cardboard (such as a cereal box)
Brown wrapping paper
18-cm yellow rickrack
1-mm needle
1 meter of white sewing thread
    and 1 meter of black sewing thread
Piece of yellow or green felt 5 cm by 4.5 cm

Small needle, 2 straight pins,
   and 2 safety pins for the kit
Notepaper strips 5 mm wide as follows:

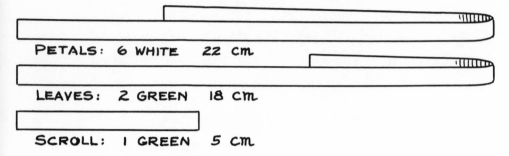

PETALS: 6 WHITE   22 CM

LEAVES: 2 GREEN   18 CM

SCROLL: 1 GREEN   5 CM

What You Do

1. From the light cardboard cut a rectangle 6 cm wide and 15 cm long. On it draw the lines that you see on the pattern. These lines are where folds are needed.

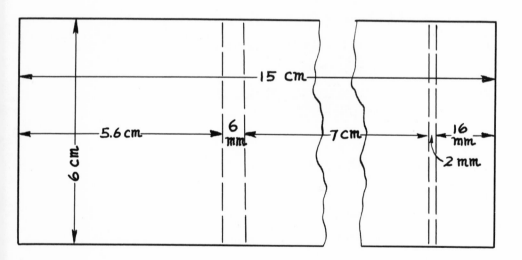

2. To get even folds, lay a ruler edge along each line. Using the points of closed scissors, make a light groove

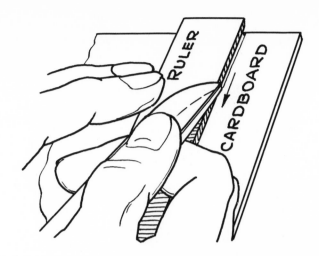

on each line. Now fold the cardboard on these grooved lines. (This is called scoring.)

3. Cut a brown wrapping-paper covering for the folded cardboard rectangle. Make it 6 cm wide and 15.5 cm long. (This covering is longer than the cardboard because it has two bends to travel around.) Glue the cover around the folded rectangle. Using a thin coat of glue, begin the covering process at the end with the narrow fold. Trim off any excess.

4. Using the 1-mm needle, wind the six white petal strips into closed round coils having a diameter of 1.5 cm. Pinch them in three places to form heart-shaped petals.

5. Make a pencil dot where the center of the flower should be on the cover of the kit. Glue the petals around this point. Dab glue under them and on their sides where they touch. Leave no spaces between them, so the flower will be compact and sturdy.

6. Make the two leaves and the two scrolls, and glue

them on by dabbing glue under them where they touch the petals.

7. Add a yellow paper-punch circle over the flower's center.

8. Insert the emergency needles and pins in the yellow (or green) felt rectangle.

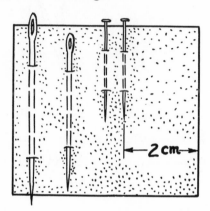

9. Cut a cardboard rectangle 4.5 cm by 5 cm, and with scissors make two parallel pairs of notches on the long sides. Leave 2 cm between one end and the first set of notches to allow room to fasten the holder into the kit. Wind a meter of black sewing thread around one set of notches and a meter of white on the other set.

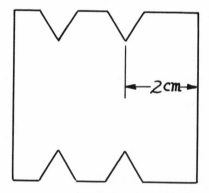

10. Slip the thread holder inside the lip made by the narrow fold of the cardboard.

11. Lay the felt needle-and-pin holder on top of the thread holder.

12. Staple through all four layers as shown.

13. Add the rickrack braid across the top and bottom to finish off the decoration.

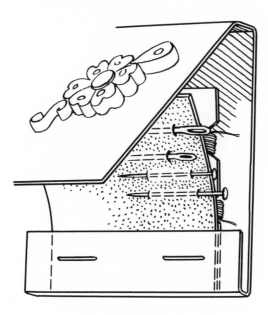

Trinket Box Lid

There are many times when we need a small gift to take to a friend as a token of our friendship or love. A trinket box with a colorful quilled lid fills such a need. Trinket boxes are fun to receive and fun to make.

Many plain-colored circular containers are available

to choose from. If the one you choose has a flexible plastic snap-on lid, you will have to replace the flexible lid with a stiff cardboard cover that will hold a quilled design. A flexible lid would flex the design off.

Cut out one cardboard circle that is slightly larger than the container. Cut two more that will just fit inside the rim. Glue the three circles together as shown.

The bird design was made from pastel, lined notebook filler paper. The lines of this paper show on the coils and provide an interesting edge tint. You can substitute other lightweight papers if you wish. You could even make the design in all white.

What You Need
2-mm needle
6-mm round pencil for winding
Cardboard for cardboard circles
Horizontal strips of lined notebook paper as follows
(Most lined paper has spaces about 5 mm wide.
They can be 7 mm. Standard paper width is 21 cm.):
50 light-green strips for border
4 light-blue strips for bird
4 yellow strips for bird
1 orange strip for bill and feet
3 pink strips for flowers

What You Do

1. First make two light-blue 40-cm strips and two yellow 40-cm strips. They are needed for the bird's head and body. For each long strip join two horizontal notebook strips end-to-end by overlapping them 1 cm. Spread glue lightly where they overlap, and allow the strips to dry thoroughly while you make the border.

→| 1 cm |← OVERLAP

21 cm ⎸ ⎸ 21 cm

The Border

2. For the first border coil, wind two green strips together around a 6-mm pencil, and let the coil pop to dime size. When you roll two strips together, the outer strip is shorter when you finish, so before you glue the tail of the outer strip, clip 2 cm off the inner strip. Pinch the coil once.

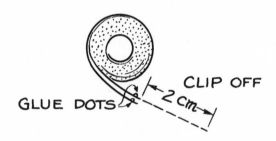

CLIP OFF

GLUE DOTS ⟍ 2 cm

3. Before you glue the first border coil in place, make a pencil dot in the exact center of the cover. Place glue under the border coil, and position it so that it points toward the pencil dot and so its rounded end extends 5 mm over the edge. As you glue each border coil in

54

place, dab glue under it and where it touches the next coil. The overhanging rounded ends form a sturdy scalloped edge for your lid, and they hide the scissor-cut edge.

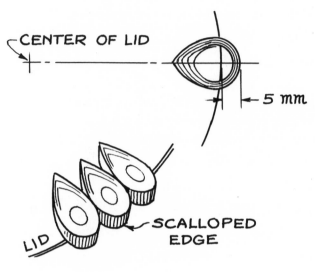

The Body

4. Before you wind the bird's body, make four narrow slashes 3 cm deep in one end of a 40-cm yellow strip. Make four slashes 2 cm deep in a long blue strip.

| YELLOW | 40 cm | |
| BLUE | 40 cm | |

5. Lay the yellow strip on top of the blue strip, with the unfringed ends flush, and wind them together around the 6-mm pencil (blue on the outside as you wind). You will have a coil the size of a quarter. Do *not* clip the inner

strip. Dab glue under the inner strip where its fringe begins, and press it to the coil. Dab glue where the blue fringe begins, and press it to the coil. The fringe forms tail feathers.

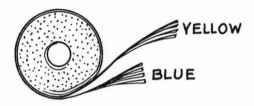

6. Glue the body coil in the center of the cover disc.

The Head

7. Before you wind the head coil, make slashes 2 cm deep in the second blue 40-cm strip. Clip 1 cm off the remaining long yellow strip, and make slashes 2 cm deep.

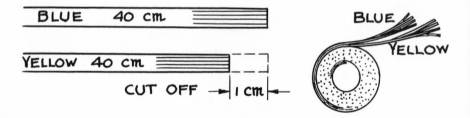

8. Lay the yellow strip on top of the blue strip, wind them together, and glue them as you did the body strips. The head coil will be the size of a dime. When you glue the head in place on the lid, make sure that the plume feathers are pointing in a clockwise direction.

The Feet

9. Cut the orange strip lengthwise to make two nar-

56

row strips. Wind one strip around the pencil, and form a dime-sized frame coil. Glue the end, and squeeze the coil into an arrow shape. Glue the feet in place.

The Beak

10. Cut an 8-cm strip off the remaining narrow orange strip, and roll the 8-cm piece around the 2-mm needle to make a 5-mm round closed coil. Squeeze the coil flat, and glue the resulting beak in place.

Flowers

11. Cut the three pink notebook strips lengthwise to make six narrow strips. Wind these six strips into small petal coils. Tuck them in place where you think they look nice.

Curly-cues: If you wish to cover the cardboard with a more pleasing texture, cover the top circle with fabric or paper before you glue the layers together. To do so, lay the top circle on the wrong side of the covering, and trace around it with a soft (#2) pencil. Make a second pencil circle about 1 cm outside the first one. With scissors make slashes about 1 cm apart, from the outer penciled line in to the inner circle. The slashes make tabs. Spread glue on these tabs, and bend them over the edge of the top circle. Do not add glue to the center of the covering, because these glue spots may cause puckers. Now you are ready to glue the three cardboard layers together.

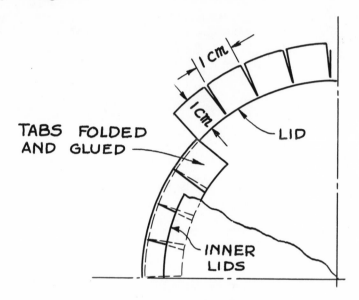

Rickrack braid or a row of paper-punch cutouts make a nice edge border for a quilled trinket box.

There are many other designs you could use beside the ones shown. Alternate possibilities are shown.

Quilled Letters

In the Middle Ages all stories and papers were copied by hand in monasteries. To make their books colorful, monks spent many hours designing and painting the first letter of the important pages. This letter was boldly outlined, and the wider parts were filled with small, bright brushstrokes. You can make your initial look very much like an illuminated letter by outlining it and using quillery in place of paint.

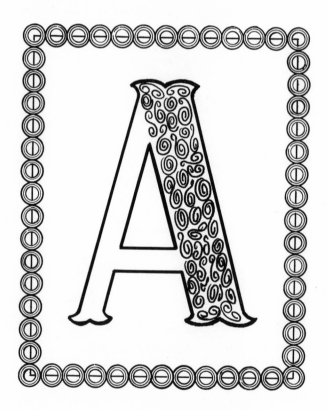

Such an initial might look nice on the cover of an important notebook. You can find interesting letters in magazines or newspapers. Or you can sign out a library book that shows different kinds of lettering.

What You Need
Fine-tipped, black-felt pen
Rectangle of heavy white paper 8 cm by 10 cm
Tweezers
1-mm needle
2-mm needle
Supply of multicolored notepaper strips
  (different lengths but *same* widths):

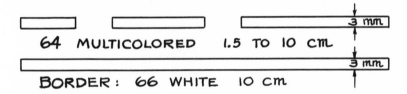

What You Do
1. Sketch your initial on the paper rectangle with a #2 pencil, leaving a border of 1.5 cm all around. Outline the letter with the felt-tip pen.

2. Using the 1-mm needle and the 2-mm needle, make the tiny colored scrolls that will fill in the wider part of your initials. Some should be S-scrolls, some should be V-scrolls, some should be eyeglass scrolls, and some should be tiny, round-open-coil scrolls.

3. Hold the coil with tweezers while you apply glue with a toothpick. With the tweezers, position the scrolls

inside your outline. Do not let the coils extend over the bold outline. Glue the coils on in a random color pattern.

4. When you have filled in the wide part of your initial, glue the rectangle on the notebook cover. Use the glue sparingly, because too much glue may cause your white background paper to pucker.

5. Use the white-notepaper strips to make white solid coils measuring 5 mm in diameter, and place them along the edge of the paper rectangle to hide it. This border is sturdy and will protect the quilled letter.

Curly-cues: You may prefer to cut out your initial in white, glue it on a colored rectangle, and then add a colorful quilled strip in the wide part. Light coils are attractive on a dark letter. You can even fill in block letters with a random quilled pattern. On some posters (depending on the theme), it is eye-catching to quill some of the key words.

May Baskets

Start your baskets in April so they will be ready on the first of May to deliver to senior citizens and shut-ins. Elderly people will be particularly happy to see this delightful custom revived. Shown in this chapter are two baskets. The first one is small and is made from a section of papier-mâché egg carton. It can hold nuts or small candy mints. The second is large and is made from a foamed-plastic cup. It can hold larger candies or cookies.

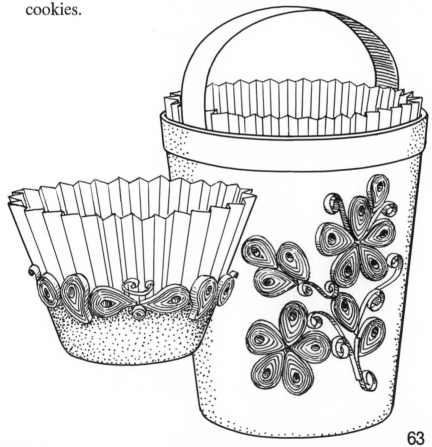

THE SMALL BASKET

What You Need

Section from a colored papier-mâché egg carton
Cupcake paper, tea cake size
1-mm needle
Narrow notepaper strips as shown:

FLOWERS: 12 OF VARIOUS COLORS   15 CM

TENDRILS: SEVERAL OF VARIOUS GREENS   3 CM

What You Do

1. Cut off one section from an egg carton, and lightly pencil a line around it 2.5 cm from the bottom. With scissors cut along this line.

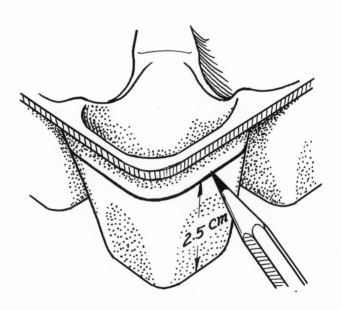

2.5 cm

2. Cut the bottom from a tea-cupcake paper. With a toothpick, spread glue around the outside top edge of the papier-mâché cup, and drop the cup inside the cupcake-paper ring. The entire basket should be about 3 cm deep.

3. Make the flower coils with the 1-mm needle. The smaller they are, the better they will look. They can be different shapes. Glue them around the cup where the two kinds of paper overlap. To hide the joint further, add tiny green tendrils between the flowers.

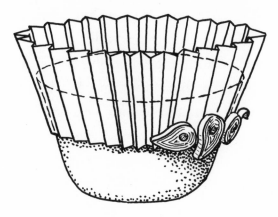

THE LARGE BASKET

What You Need
White foamed-plastic cup, such as disposable beverage
   cup
Pastel-colored cupcake paper
Bright ribbon for handle, about 20 cm
2-mm needle
6 snap clothespins

Notepaper strips 3 mm wide as follows:

FLOWERS: 15 PASTEL 22 cm

LEAVES: 9 GREEN 15 cm

SCROLLS: 8 YELLOW 4 cm

What You Do

1. Glue the ribbon's ends inside the cup, taking up about 3 cm on each end. Be sure ends are on opposite sides of the cup. Let them dry well.

2. Cut the bottom (the uncrimped part) from the cupcake paper. So that this crimped ring will stretch enough to fit the top of your cup, you will need to make eight slashes, 1 cm deep, around the lower edge of the cupcake paper.

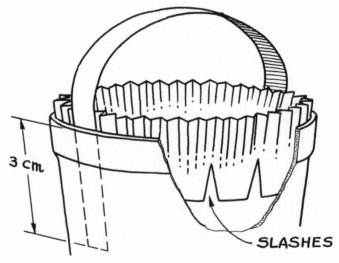

3 cm

SLASHES

3. With a wooden toothpick, spread glue around the inside edge of the cup, and drop the crimped ring into the cup. Press the cupcake paper in place so that about 1 cm of it shows above the cup. The cupcake paper is waxy. The foamed-plastic cup also has a waxlike surface. White craft glue will bond these two materials together, but it will take longer than bonding a thirsty paper to foamed plastic. To keep the cupcake paper against the inside edge of the cup while the glue dries, clip six snap clothespins around the cup.

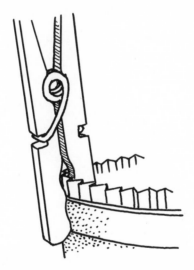

4. Wind the fifteen pastel petals on the 2-mm needle, and position them on the cup. Before the glue sets make certain they are centered on the area between the handle ends.

5. Wind the leaves and glue them in place.

6. Then tuck scrolls in the spaces that seem to need them to balance the design.

7. You might want to crush a paper napkin and push it into the bottom of the cup to cushion the treats you plan to add.

Curly-cues: Save leftover coils in a small container. In another container save very short leftover strips. Both kinds of scraps can be used on May baskets.

The baskets may be decorated with a border design, such as one using small scrolls.

If you should wish to include curving, graceful, long stems in your design, you may use green yarn for them. You may also make a yarn handle by braiding nine strands of green yarn.

Pierre, A Pet French Poodle

A poodle makes a pert decoration for a lampshade or a desk letter basket. He can be black, tan, white, gray, or even light blue or purple. He can wear sequins or bows or whatever you like.

The size of a poodle's curls varies. On his ears and scalp they are tiny while his shoulder and chest sections have large curls. You can show this fur texture by rolling some tiny strips on needles of different sizes. You can cut some strips narrower than others. And you can alter his fur texture even further by gluing on some of the coils upright and laying others horizontal.

For a lampshade ornament, complete Pierre first as a cutout, and then fix him to the shade. Once on his background, you can add some grass and flowers.

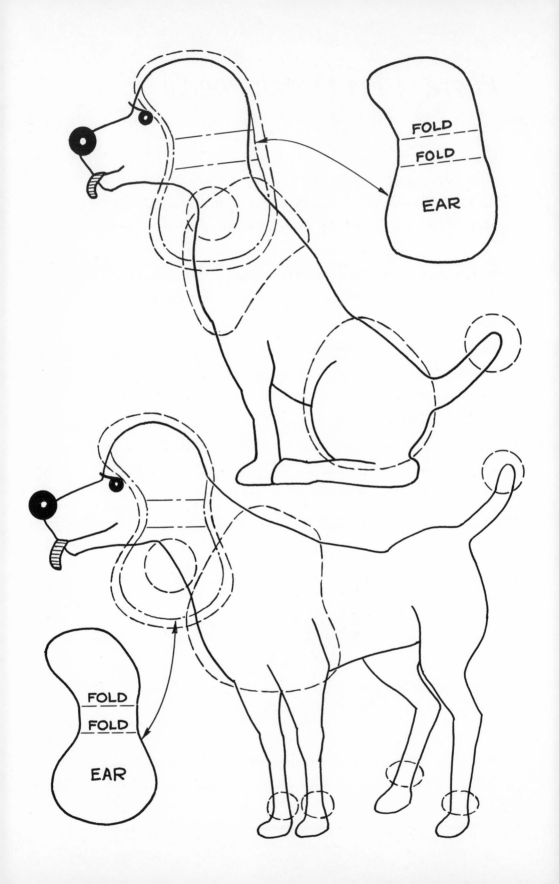

FOLD
FOLD

EAR

FOLD
FOLD

EAR

What You Need (for a white poodle):

1-mm needle

2-mm needle

Heavy white paper for body cutout

Notepaper strips as follows:

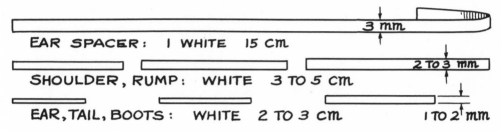

Construction paper strips as follows:

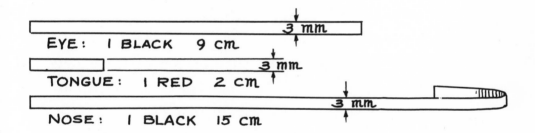

What You Do

Trace the dog pattern you wish to use, following the instructions on pages 27-28. Transfer the ear/scalp and body outline to the piece of heavy white paper. Carefully cut out the two parts.

The Ear/Scalp Cutout and Eye

1. Lightly sketch in the dotted lines on the ear cutout. These are lines for folds that will make the ear

71

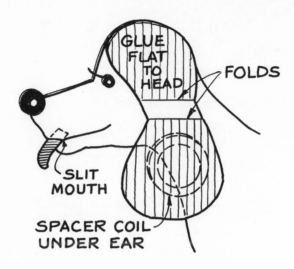

GLUE FLAT TO HEAD

FOLDS

SLIT MOUTH

SPACER COIL UNDER EAR

stand out away from the body. Notice that the scalp end of this cutout is the part that is attached to the head.

2. First lay a ruler edge under the cutout where the lower dotted line is drawn. Bend the scalp end away from you.

3. Now place the ruler edge on top of the cutout along the upper line. This time bend the scalp end toward you. With your fingers sharpen these folds.

4. To keep the ear flap permanently in a raised position, coil the 15-cm under-ear strip into a round, closed, dime-sized coil.

5. Glue it on the ear flap so it will be hidden inside when the flap is folded.

6. Lightly spread glue under the scalp end of the cutout, and adhere it in place on the dog's head.

7. The eye is made and glued in place next, so the head curls can come right up to it and maybe cover part of it. You want him to appear to be peeping from under

his curls. Roll the 9-cm black strip into a tight coil, using the 1-mm needle. Dab glue about 5 mm from the tail end, and press this spot against the coil. The extending 5-mm tail will make eyelashes. The eye should then be glued in place. Make sure his lashes point upward, and make sure his eye is level with the top of his muzzle.

8. Now add the curls to the poodle's head. Make some with the 1-mm needle and some with the 2-mm needle. As you roll each tiny narrow scroll, hold it with tweezers while you lightly apply glue under it with a toothpick and while you lay it in place.

9. Allow some coils to extend slightly beyond the outline to suggest unruly curls.

The Nose and Tongue

10. Make the nose by winding the 15-cm black strip into a round tight coil. A real poodle's nose is like a rounded button that sits on the end of his muzzle. So when you glue the nose coil on the dog's head, position it so that it extends a bit above and beyond the outline.

11. The tongue strip needs to be rounded slightly at one end and the tip rolled on the 2-mm needle so that it barely curls. Make a tiny slit where the dog's mouth begins. Dab the unrolled tongue end with glue, and slip it under the jaw slit.

The Shoulder-Chest Section (*and Rump*)

12. Make some of the shoulder curls with the wider strips and the 1-mm needle. Make some with the 2-mm needle. Vary the widths of the strips. If most of these coils are wider than the head coils, they will add depth

and interest. Glue some on vertically and glue some on horizontally to give his fur a natural appearance. Be sure the curls extend slightly over the edges of the outline.

The Tail and Boots

13. Use the 1-mm needle for most of the boot and tail coils to suggest that on these body parts the curls have been clipped. Lay some vertically and some horizontally.

Gluing Pierre on His Background

14. Carefully spread glue on the underside of the dog, and press him on the lampshade where he looks best. To establish a base line, place some flowers and bits of grass near his feet.

Curly-cues: The standing Pierre can have two or three sequins or beads added in the section between his shoulder curls and his scalp to suggest a collar.

Lavender coils or light-pink coils, on a darker shade of the same color, give poodles a Parisian look!

Place Cards

Place cards with quilling can add interest and a holiday touch to your dinner table. Choose a design to fit the occasion. Here are two informal spring designs—a chicken and a rabbit—and two formal ideas—a quilled flower and a design that combines quilling with cutout fruit.

The size of place cards may vary. They may be folded so they will stand like the one in the picture, or they may be unfolded cards as small as 5 cm by 9 cm.

FLOWER DESIGN

What You Need
Heavy white paper for the place card
1-mm needle
Notepaper strips 3 mm wide, the lengths shown:

FLOWER CENTER: 3 YELLOW 8 cm

PETALS: 8 DARK RED 20 cm

STEM: 1 GREEN 6 cm

LEAVES: 2 GREEN 20 cm

What You Do

1. Make a pencil mark near the upper left corner of the place card where you think the center of the flower should be.

2. Using the 1-mm needle, roll the yellow strips into three tight cylindrical coils, and glue them over the pencil mark in a triangular cluster.

3. With the 1-mm needle, roll the eight dark-red strips into round tight coils. Glue them around the three central coils. They should be evenly spaced and resting on their rims like wheels ready to roll.

4. Fold the green stem strip into a V. With a toothpick, lightly spread glue inside it and under it. Press its sides together. Attach it to the card so that its tip slides between two of the red petals.

5. Roll the two leaf strips into round tight coils. Dab

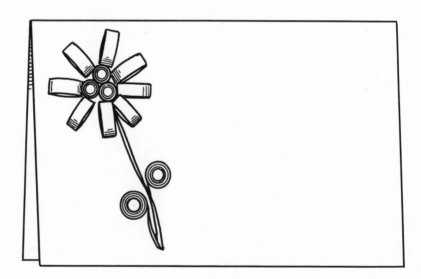

glue under them and on the spots where they will touch the stem. Place a leaf on each side of the stem to give it strength.

Curly-cue: This flower can be made in yellow or pink for a spring card. It is pretty on a large card when two or three blossoms branch from the same stem.

FRUIT DESIGN

What You Need
Plain card for place card
1-mm needle
Notepaper for 3-mm strips and cutouts:

GRAPES: 20 PURPLE OR BLUE   APPLE SPACER: 1 RED 14 cm

LEAF: 1 GREEN   PEAR SPACER: 2 YELLOW 12 cm

SCROLLS: 6 GREEN   4 cm

What You Do
1. Follow the patterns on the next page. Using a quarter and a dime as tracing aids, draw and cut out the rounded fruits. Make the banana 5.5 cm long. Draw and cut out a grape leaf like the one shown.
2. Glue the banana on first and then add the orange, leaving a 3-mm space between them.

3. Wind the red strip into a coil slightly smaller than dime size and glue it to the underside of the red-apple cutout. Glue this raised apple on top of the banana and orange.

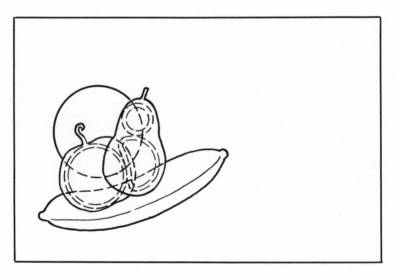

4. Coil one yellow strip into a round closed coil that will fit under the top part of the pear.

5. Coil the second yellow strip into a closed coil and squeeze it into a D-shape. Glue this coil under the bottom part of the pear.

78

6. With a 1-mm needle, make and add a pinched coil for a leaf on top of the banana, close to the pear.

7. The grapes are solid tight coils (blue or purple) about 3 mm in diameter. Use the 1-mm needle to make them. The first layer needs twelve grapes, and the second layer needs eight grapes.

8. Add the grape leaf and the tendrils.

CHICKEN DESIGN

What You Need
2-mm needle
Notepaper strips the widths and lengths shown:

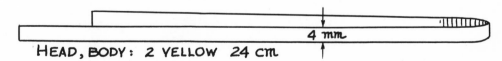

4 mm

HEAD, BODY: 2 YELLOW 24 CM

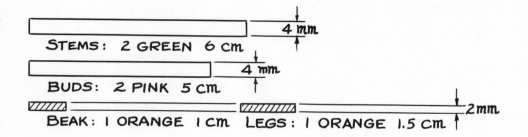

STEMS: 2 GREEN 6 CM 4 mm

BUDS: 2 PINK 5 CM 4 mm

BEAK: 1 ORANGE 1 CM LEGS: 1 ORANGE 1.5 CM 2mm

What You Do

1. Wind one yellow strip into a dime-sized round closed coil for the head. Dab glue under it and position it near the upper left corner of the card. Before the glue sets, push the needle hole to the spot where you think the eye should be.

2. Wind the other yellow strip into a quarter-sized round closed coil, dab glue under it and where it touches the head, and fix it to the card.

3. Bend the two tiny orange bits into a beak and legs. Glue them in place.

4. Make two small V scrolls for stems, and glue them near the chick's feet. (Be sure you leave room for the guest's name.) Once the stems are in place, add two tiny pink buds on top of them.

RABBIT DESIGN

What You Need
1-mm needle
Notepaper strips 4 mm wide as shown:

TAIL: 1 LIGHT BLUE 6 cm

EARS, LEGS: 4 PINK 20 cm

FEET: 2 LIGHT BLUE 20 cm

HEAD, BODY: 2 LIGHT BLUE 24 cm

What You Do
The Body

1. Wind a light-blue strip into the body coil, and pinch one end. Before pinching, this coil should be 1 cm in diameter. Because the strip is fairly long and is wound on a 1-mm needle, it will have lots of spring. But letting it open to 1 cm only gives the body an almost solid look. Glue this coil to the card near the left side but about halfway between the top and bottom.

The Head and Ears

2. Wind the other 24-cm blue strip into a head coil. Make it into a closed round coil, 1 cm in diameter, before pinching it. Position it with the pinched tip pointing up a little to give the rabbit a jaunty air.

3. Next wind and glue on the two pinched-coil ears.

The Legs and Feet

4. Wind the two legs the size of those in the picture. Glue them on so that they touch each other at the top and so they also touch the body coil. One should point slightly forward and one slightly backward.

5. Wind the two feet coils. When you glue them in place, point the back foot downward a little and point the front foot upward a little to suggest motion.

The Tail

6. Add the tail at the back of the body. Position it on the body so that it almost touches the back leg.

7. Add a couple of buds near the rabbit's feet.

Curly-cues: Both the rabbit and the chicken could be used on a baby card or on an Easter egg. Either of them would look attractive as a decoration on a rock paperweight.

You could make a plumed bird instead of the chicken.

In place of a 24-cm yellow strip, wind a 12-cm blue strip with a 12-cm yellow strip and fringe the ends of the strips. A plumed bird does not have to be yellow or blue. It could be made with two strips of red. Or green.

For your school bazaar why not make up some matching sets of place cards? A flat design similar to the bracelet design would allow you to stack a set of eight cards into a nice neat package to sell.

Christmas Wreath

Among your used holiday cards look for a printed greeting that is compact enough to show through an opening 5 cm or 6 cm in diameter. Make a wreath to frame the printed greeting. When completed, your wreath can be a package decoration or be hung on your tree.

What You Need
Printed greeting
Green background paper for wreath
1-mm needle

2-mm needle

Notepaper strips of various lengths and widths
as shown:

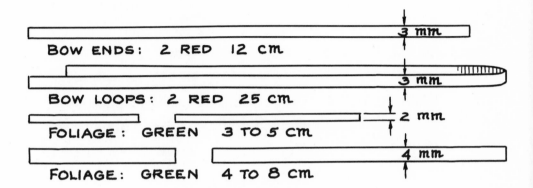

BOW ENDS: 2 RED 12 CM   3 mm

BOW LOOPS: 2 RED 25 CM   3 mm

FOLIAGE: GREEN 3 TO 5 CM   2 mm

FOLIAGE: GREEN 4 TO 8 CM   4 mm

What You Do

1. From the green background paper cut a circle 8 cm in diameter.

2. Draw a circle about 6 cm in diameter around your greeting.

3. Cut out the circular greeting and glue it on the center of the 8-cm green circle.

4. Make the green foliage strips into scrolls of different shapes. Coil some of them with the 1-mm needle and some with the 2-mm needle. If the foliage coils are of different heights, they will give the greenery a more natural texture. Using tweezers and a toothpick to apply glue, lay the coils on the wreath in a random pattern. Allow some of the coils to extend over the edges to hide the scissor-cut ridge.

5. Using the 2-mm needle roll the two 25-cm red strips into two round closed coils the size of a nickel.

Then pinch them in three places to form triangular coils. Roll the two 12-cm strips into dime-sized coils. Form these into triangles. Arrange these four coils on top of the wreath to form a bow at the four-o'clock position. After gluing them in place, add a red paper-punch cut-out for a knot in the center of the bow.

Curly-cues: If you wish, you may use your photograph inside the wreath. Or you may use a tiny holiday scene that pleases you. You could even use white strips to represent snowy boughs.

If you are planning to mail your wreath, glue the red bow on first. Then fill in around it with scrolls made from strips all cut the *same* widths, in order to keep the wreath flat.

Coils glued on in an upright position are really small cylinders. They are strong and, when they are the same height and evenly distributed over a surface, will hold considerable pressure without crushing. To help distribute the force of any blows your wreath will receive in mailing, slip a rectangle of light cardboard on top of it when you slip it into its envelope.

Snowflake Designs

Quilled snowflakes, if made with care, make beautiful tree ornaments or package decorations.

If you wish to make several the same size, make a template of a six-pointed star first. Whiten a supply of flat wooden toothpicks and precut your stars and strips. But cut carefully. Be exact so your snowflakes will have symmetry.

What You Need for Both Star A and Star B
Cardboard for template
White cardboard for star
Flat wooden toothpicks
White paint
2-mm needle
Strips, 4 mm wide, of heavy white typing paper as shown:

STAR B: 6 WHITE 7 cm

STAR A: 18 WHITE   STAR B: 16 WHITE   20 cm

What You Do to Make Star A
1. Paint six wooden toothpicks with white paint. While they are drying, trace the star pattern and make a template.

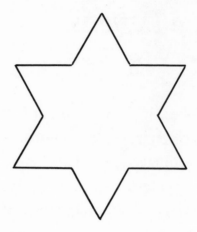

2. Make nine strips 38 cm long by pairing eighteen of the 20-cm strips and joining them end-to-end.

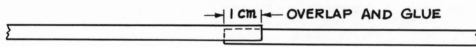

3. While the glued strips and painted toothpicks dry, prepare the white-cardboard star. To do so, trace around your star template, following the instruction on page 28, and cut out along your outline.

4. Wind one of the dry 38-cm strips around the 2-mm needle into a tight closed coil, measuring 1 cm in diameter. Glue this coil in the *exact* center of the white cardboard star.

5. Glue a white toothpick through each of the six star points. The wide ends of the toothpicks must touch the center coil. Check the positions of the toothpicks before the glue sets. Also check to be certain that the distances between the outer tips of the toothpicks are equal.

6. Using a 2-mm needle and eight 38-cm strips, wind eight round closed coils the size of a dime. Size these coils to make sure they are identical. Then pinch them at both ends to make eight eye-shaped coils.

7. After pinching the coils, size them again to see if they are identical in size, shape, and inner design. Glue the best *six* eye shapes in place. Their inner points should touch the center coil. Each eye shape should be centered along a toothpick, and each outer point should rest on a point of the star.

8. To make the six small closed coils, use six 20-cm strips. Each coil must have a diameter of .5 cm. Before tucking them in place between the eye shapes, dab glue under them and on their sides where they will touch the eye-shaped coils. This step will strengthen the whole structure.

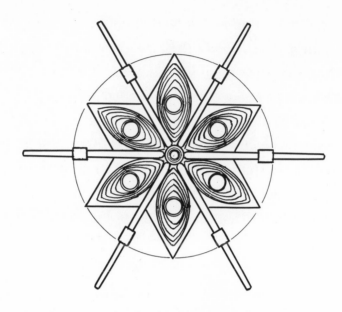

What You Do to Make Star B

1. Paint six wooden toothpicks with white paint. While they are drying, trace the star pattern and cut it out.

2. Join sixteen 20-cm strips to make eight 38-cm strips. Let them dry.

3. Make your template and star as in instructions for Star A.

4. While the long strips dry, roll one of the 20-mm strips into a round closed coil .5 in diameter. Glue it in the *exact* center of the star.

5. Note that on Star B each toothpick divides a valley between two star peaks. Glue the six toothpicks in place, making certain that they touch the central coil and that the distances between the outer ends are equal.

6. Using the 2-mm needle and eight of the dry 38-cm

strips, construct eight dime-sized round closed coils. After sizing them, pinch both ends to form eight eye-shaped coils. Select the best six to glue in the diamond-shaped sections that show between the toothpicks.

7. For the six small tight coils near the outer ends of the toothpicks, you need six 7-cm strips. Make light pencil marks on the toothpicks where you wish the out-side edge of each coil to be located. Glue the starting end of each strip to a toothpick at the pencil mark, and wind the strips by hand into tight closed coils. Glue the end.

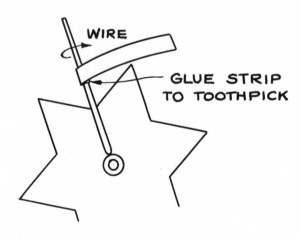

WIRE

GLUE STRIP
TO TOOTHPICK

Curly-cues: For snowflakes that glisten, sprinkle on a little glitter. For snowflakes with luster, tiny white pearls can be tucked into the holes left by the needle.

To make smaller stars, construct a six-pointed star inside a smaller circle, use smaller strips, and a 1-mm needle.

The most beautiful snowflake stars (or other geometric designs) are those that are not mounted on a cardboard background. Some examples are given here. Such designs can be quite strong if you assemble your coils well and if care is taken to glue each coil where it touches the others around it. When assembling these delicate designs, work on a clear plastic lid that is centered over the concentric circle drawing.

Some More Curly-cues

On Easter eggs quillery can look much like bits of candy and colored icing. Braid trimming, paper dots, and tiny pearls can be added too.

Bugs, bees, and fish can be three-dimensional eye-catchers for ecology posters.

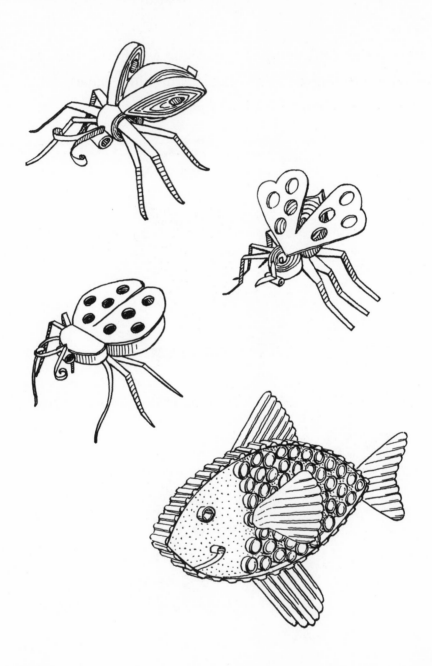

A piggy bank can be made by covering a jug or an inflated balloon with papier-mâché. Pink or peach paint makes a good background for coils. A piggy bank can serve as a sampler for displaying all the flowers you have learned to make. Swags of tiny rickrack or rows of paper dots help to make this sampler more colorful.

There's no end to the many uses you will find for curled paper coils!